How Ch Pastors, and Professionals Are Partnering with a Team to Write a Book, Get Published, and Redeem Culture

Caleb Breakey

sermontobook
.com

Copyright © 2021 by **Caleb Breakey**

All rights reserved. No part of this publication may be reproduced, distributed, or transmitted in any form or by any means, without prior written permission.

Speak It To Book, for Christian Leaders and Professionals
www.speakittobook.com

Sermon To Book, for Christian Pastors
www.sermontobook.com

Renown Publishing
www.renownpublishing.com

How Christian Leaders, Pastors, and Professionals Are Partnering with a Team to Write a Book, Get Published, and Redeem Culture
Caleb Breakey

ISBN-13: 978-1-952602-51-1

CONTENTS

3 Questions to Determine If You Should Write Your Book ... 3

How We Transform Your Stories, Ideas, or Sermons into a Book 7

What Your Peers Are Saying About Speak It To Book and Sermon To Book 17

FAQ: Is Speak It To Book or Sermon To Book Right for Me? 23

FAQ: How Do Speak It To Book and Sermon To Book Work? 25

FAQ: How Are Speak It To Book and Sermon To Book Different from Other Publishers? 29

FAQ: How Much of My Time and Energy Is Required? 31

Meet Caleb Breakey 33

CHAPTER ONE

3 Questions to Determine If You Should Write Your Book

Are you an image-bearer of Jesus ready to step into the harvest and do fruitful work that matters to God and the world?

Do you possess a holy ambition to expose harm, recapture truth, and bring hope to the world through paradigm-shifting ideas and transparency?

Do you desire to magnify the virtuous and mitigate the vain through the power of story and counter-cultural narratives?

Then you not only should but *must* write your book.

My name is Caleb Breakey, and I own and operate Speak It To Book and Sermon To Book, Christian companies devoted to producing, publishing, and positioning books for Jesus-loving leaders, pastors, and professionals.

I spent a decade breaking into traditional publishing but only managed to sell 20K books. So, I stopped writing for 4 years to learn platform-building from a billion-dollar advertising master. What good was a message, after all, if you couldn't get it out to the world? Now I serve as the Director of HarperCollins Christian Publishing's coaching program for aspiring authors, Author Gateway, and I've helped hundreds of authors write books, hit numerous best-seller lists (New York Times, Wall Street Journal, USA Today, #1 book on all of Amazon), build 6-figure author platforms, win contracts, and transform the world.

The words I long to hear at the end of my life were penned many hundreds of years before my birth in Numbers 14:24 (NKJV): "But My servant Caleb, because he has a different spirit in him and has followed Me fully, I will bring into the land."

If you desire to restore culture to what it was always meant to be by blessing others through sacrifice...

If you are open to sharing your most authentic self with the world and find sacredness in meeting others in their present state...

And if you want to do meaningful work that produces transformation in the thoughts and beliefs of people...

Then this short book is a must-read for you.

Our mission at Speak It To Book and Sermon To Book is to redeem culture through *you* by transforming the years you've invested into your ministry, career, or business into a soul-impacting book and far-reaching author platform.

An author platform is a system that helps you start a relationship between you and your ideal readers every day. Developing a solid author platform prepares you to influence thousands of lives—if not *tens* of thousands.

We believe...

- That publishing the right authors has the uncanny ability to initiate redemptive possibilities, restore souls from idolatry and injustice, and bend the spiritual direction of society.

- That positioning the right authors—spiritually serious, culturally astute—has the power to demonstrate Christ's fearless love to the nations.

- That committing one's talents and resources to bringing beauty and justice into places of brokenness will shape future generations to become fully alive in the work of God's kingdom.

In short, your stories, ideas, and sermons should be impacting lives, not collecting brain dust.

What if you had a way to overcome your busy schedule and get all those ideas out of your head?

What if you could partner with a team to end procrastination, write your book, and take that next step into significance?

A partnership with Speak It To Book or Sermon To Book surrounds you with literary professionals to guide you through the work of producing, positioning, and publishing your book—without overloading your schedule.

So, if you don't know how to write your book or find your voice, or you don't know how the publishing industry works or how to navigate your options, our team can help you:

- Capture the mission and vision of your book and use it as a resource to exhort, equip, and empower readers.

- Architect your author platform and position you to build relationships strategically with souls who need your book.

- Make introductions to literary agents and major publishing houses so you can be considered for a traditional book deal.

CHAPTER TWO

How We Transform Your Stories, Ideas, or Sermons into a Book

Interviews

We start by drawing out the message that's been bursting inside of you. This includes meetings to set goals, clear up foggy ideas, form your book's table of contents, and thoroughly extract and structure your stories, ideas, and wisdom.

Ghostwriting, Review, and Approval

We develop your content into draft chapters that read like a fluid, concise, powerful book, and then send them to you for review. This ensures we're capturing the written style you desire and are producing your intended message.

Workbook

At the end of each chapter, we add what we call a "workbook." These sections include questions to help readers interact with your content via question prompts.

Title and Back Cover Copy

We choose a strategic title to hook your audience, write engaging back cover copy that speaks to their unique struggle, and then lay out your book's benefits so your readership feels seen, heard, and understood.

Design and Formatting

We collaborate with you to create the best cover for your book based on other best-selling titles in your category. We then format your book for both eBook and paperback distribution.

The Full Rough Draft of Your Book

A few months prior to publication, we send you a full draft of your book. We then work with you to conduct two major rounds of feedback and edits.

Proofreading and Citation

Readers expect a published work to be free of mistakes. We do, too. We also help to cite your quoted or paraphrased sources as endnotes and verify the verbatim accuracy of scriptural quotations.

Positioning for Platform Growth

Our process for growing your author platform centers on these 4 elements: Assets, Relationship, Pipeline, and Tracking.

1) **Assets** means writing your books and creating your web pages—which we refer to as an "online funnel"—so that you can systematically deliver valuable content to your readers.

2) **Relationship** means automating the relationship-building process with your readership through a strategic email sequence, which allows you to connect with each reader on a personal level without draining you of time or energy.

3) **Pipeline** means making sure new readers are finding your book every day via paid advertising, which ensures that your work is consistently discoverable, and your author platform is constantly growing.

4) **Tracking** means determining the true cost of impacting souls long after your launch week so that you can work toward building a sustainable writing ministry.

Publication Options

The following is a high-level overview of our Speak It To Book and Sermon To Book packages, which we broadly split into "Self-Publishing" packages and "Traditional Publishing" packages. These paths are designed for Christian leaders, pastors, and professionals who want to pen a professional book in their voice and words—but don't have the time or energy to dedicate to writing.

Self-Publishing: *Keep Your Intellectual Property, Earn 100% of Your Book Royalties, and* Retain Speak It To Book or Sermon To Book *as Your Publishing Partner*

If you purchase one of our Self-Publishing packages, we publish your eBook, print book, and optional audiobook via our Renown Publishing imprint. We then position you for platform growth and employ a launch strategy designed to hit best-seller status in your book's subcategory during your book's launch week. This short-term sales push opens a window of leverage to secure speaking engagements and podcast appearances that fuel post-launch buzz.

Traditional Publishing: *Sign with a Literary Agent, Earn Up to a $10,000 Advance, and Enjoy Mass Distribution with a Major Christian Publisher*

If you purchase one of our Traditional Publishing packages, we help you write an eye-popping book proposal, architect, and build the assets required to snatch the attention of industry professionals, and then introduce you and pitch your book to premier traditional publishing gatekeepers. If these efforts do not land you a literary agent or traditional book deal, we pivot to self-publishing your book via our imprint, Renown Publishing.

What's the Most Important Aspect of Your Process That Goes Overlooked?

Answer: Your book should be the *beginning* of your relationship with your readers, not the *end*.

For pastors who are looking to launch or grow their church, multiply their small groups, or introduce their church's cultural DNA, a book is the *beginning,* not the *end*—it supercharges your ability to develop, nurture, and grow a culture that aims to know God and make Him known.

For leaders and professionals who want to feed their business or entrepreneurial endeavors with warmed-up prospects, a book is the *beginning,* not the *end*—it maximizes your ability to nurture your relationship with prospects and fills your client acquisition pipeline.

You should always be asking yourself, "What's my audience's next problem after they've finished reading the book?" or "How can I speed up how fast my readers solve their problem?"

Reading alone boasts a learning retention rate of 10%.

- How might you add a product that's audiovisual (20% retention)?

- How about a video that focuses on demonstration (30% retention)?

- What about hosting online discussing groups (50% retention)?

- Or in-person workshops where your readers practice what you've preached (75% retention)?

- Or positioning your readers to teach what they've learned from your book (90% retention)?

When you have your book written and published, the possibilities for additional impact are *endless*. Put yourself in your readers' shoes, feel their pains, and then start solving them.

Use your book as a *beginning,* not an *end.*

Shouldn't I Write the Book Myself?

In short, no.

Because in our experience, that is the question keeping thousands of aspiring writers from putting pen to paper.

If you are too busy to write your book, the odds are that you have *become* the book—and that is a wonderful thing. It means you are living out what you want to write about, but you do not have the time or energy to put it on paper.

When a person has *become* their book, we find that their words bring life and transformation. We find that they are a natural teacher and encourager who inspires others with their stories and ideas. We find that their mission isn't about them—it's about *others* (redemptive work). We find that they are compassionate, driven, and ambitious.

So, why would you ever procrastinate in writing your book and building your author platform?

No one can be an excellent craftsman, editor, proofreader, designer, formatter, packager, copywriter, publisher, distributor, book launch expert, funnel builder, ad manager, automation expert, strategizer, and video producer all by themselves.

If you want to go fast, go alone.

But if you want to go far, go *together*.

I don't want you to spend a decade writing your book. I don't want you investing 4 years into learning author platform-building. I want you to write your book now so you can secure a traditional book deal like Michael Todd. Keynote to 100,000 people in two years and get featured in *Entrepreneur On Fire*, *Forbes*, and *Inc.* like John Hawkins. Sell 1,500 books during a 30-day speaking tour like Randy Borders.

Mobilize Your Mission, Multiply Your Redemptive Work, and Maximize Kingdom Impact

So, here's your next step. We offer a turnkey service where we take your stories, ideas, or sermons and turn them into books. We then build your author platform and determine the best publishing path for you—self-publishing or traditional publishing. Finally, we position you to help impact lives long after your book hits shelves.

Scan the image below or scroll to our contact info to learn how our Speak It To Book and Sermon To Book programs are changing the lives of Christian leaders, pastors, and professionals across the nation.

You've been putting off your dreams of writing and publishing for long enough. You now have insider publishing knowledge in your arsenal. You know exactly what you must do to write, publish, and impact lives with your book.

Let's make it happen.

Scan or scroll to our contact info below if you are a Christian leader, pastor, or professional and want to learn more about the Speak It To Book or Sermon To Book process.

Our team of Jesus-loving publishing professionals are friendly and easy to talk to. We would love to hear the vision for your book and answer any questions!

Phone

360-836-0672

Websites

www.speakittobook.com
www.sermontobook.com

Email

info@speakittobook.com
info@sermontobook.com

Address

Speak It To Book
424 W. Bakerview Rd. Ste. 105
#215
Bellingham, WA 98226

What Your Peers Are Saying About Speak It To Book and Sermon To Book

I had a burden to release a book, but I did not have the time or expertise to make it happen. Then I found the secret sauce: Caleb Breakey and his team at Speak It To Book.
—**Michael Todd, Pastor of Transformation Church**
Because of his book, Michael secured a traditional book deal with WaterBrook & Multnomah.

I had all this cool stuff in my head but didn't know what to do with it. Caleb and his team are the experts with this kind of problem. They are a great company to do business with and have a fantastic process for people who want to get their thoughts and ideas into a book.

—John Hawkins, Business Consultant

Because of his book, John keynoted to 100,000 in two years and was featured in Entrepreneur on Fire, Forbes, and Inc.

As an aspiring author, Caleb and his team helped me make that jump. They were able to take my vision and my idea and formulate my words to convey my message perfectly. Thank you!

—Elizabeth Cook, CEO of Integrated Being

Because of her book, Elizabeth enrolled more clients in her 90-day workshops and weekend retreats.

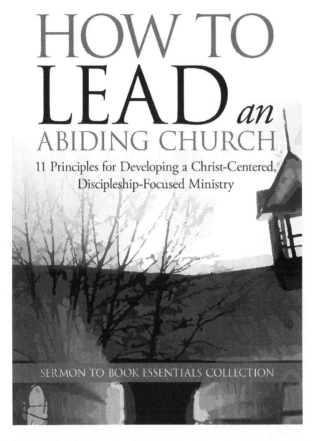

NATE SWEENEY

HOW TO LEAD *an*

ABIDING CHURCH

11 Principles for Developing a Christ-Centered, Discipleship-Focused Ministry

SERMON TO BOOK ESSENTIALS COLLECTION

Caleb Breakey and his team serve as a catalyst to the blueprint God has for your life. If you've put that content away in a file—never to be used again—then you need to get in touch with Caleb.
—Nate Sweeney, The Abiding Network Founder and Directional Leader
Because of his book, Nate grew his email list to 3,000 and started offering online workshops.

If what you have to say is worth being heard, it is worth being published. The purpose of the author is to provide the message. Caleb and his team can help deliver that message.
—Randy Borders, Pastor and Consecrated Bishop
Because of his book, Randy planned a 30-day speaking tour and achieved 2X his investment in one month.

FAQ: Is Speak It To Book or Sermon To Book Right for Me?

Speak It To Book and Sermon To Book are right for you if...

√ **...you are ready to cement your influence and legacy.** Books give your message permanence and help you transform the lives of others for years to come.

√ **...you are wanting to expand your reach and credibility.** A book can connect you to homes, offices, and inboxes that you otherwise would have never been able to reach.

√ ...you are ready to build an author platform and future with your voice. We can help you use your book as the center of your expanding influence.

√ **...you are ready for a team to take your book from good to great!** No one can write, publish, and market all alone. It's critical for you to have a strong team behind your ideas to help make your book a masterpiece.

Speak It To Book and Sermon To Book are not right for you if …

√ **…you are not ready to invest in your future.** Publishing has a cost—but the benefits make it an investment, not an expense.

√ **…you think that a book will make you rich.** Books are stepping-stones to reach more lives and build influence, *not* a shortcut to get rich fast.

√ **…you don't want a team to help you write, publish, and market your book.** A book will always be stronger with a team standing behind it. If you don't feel you need that support, we aren't for you.

√ **…you believe you can write a quality book in a short amount of time.** Inspired messages may come quickly to a person but getting them out to the rest of the world does not.

FAQ: How Do Speak It To Book and Sermon To Book Work?

Your Ideas, Our Team

We take you from ideas or sermons to published book.

No Writing Frustrations

Our system saves you time and energy so that your focus remains on your message.

No Technology Complications

Our method is designed to take away the complications of building your author platform.

No Publishing Hassle

We do everything in top-notch quality with a focused team of experts throughout the process.

Your Contribution

Foundation Call

We help you choose your book idea or sermon series, set goals, and fashion your outline.

Feedback

You provide feedback on sample chapters and drafts to make sure we capture your writing voice.

Book Launch

We celebrate your accomplishment, gain exposure, and capitalize on media attention.

Book Creation Process

Refining

Before digging into your stories, ideas, or sermons, we refine your idea until it's crystal clear.

Outlining

We use your stories, ideas, or sermon series to create an outline for your book.

Writing

We write your book using your words to connect with your ideal reader.

Launching

We launch your book to best-seller status in its subcategory on Amazon during its launch week.

Positioning

We craft your media kit and press release and coach you through getting featured on podcasts and conference stages.

Our Commitment to You

Care and Quality

We pride ourselves on our professional team of expert writers, editors, marketers, and designers. You will receive top-notch results in both care and quality.

Valuing Your Time

Our process frees you to focus on your personal priorities while still receiving the invaluable accomplishment of publishing your own book.

Integrity and Trust

We serve you with the utmost respect, integrity, and trust. We do more than just write and publish books. We build life-long client relationships.

FAQ: How Are Speak It To Book and Sermon To Book Different from Other Publishers?

Most publishers require a polished and completed manuscript. Speak It To Book and Sermon To Book *create and publish* polished and completed manuscripts.

We boast a one-of-a-kind experience that works for publishing high-quality books. Our process is the most innovative publishing experience in the world for Christian leaders, pastors, and professionals.

From the start, we guide you through every step of our process. Your book gets focused attention from professional writers, editors, designers, and marketers. Our Founder, Caleb Breakey, lives and breathes publishing and author platform building. He leads the charge so that your message can reach far beyond your current circle of influence.

FAQ: How Much of My Time and Energy Is Required?

Your time investment is dependent on how much you want to be involved in the process.

Here is a general breakdown of how you contribute through each phase of your book's development.

Foundation and Strategy Sessions (1–3 hours)

We help you formulate your big idea, strategize, and set goals.

Your Content (1–2 hours)

You'll share a 500-word sample that showcases your writing style so we can learn your true writing voice. If you have a potential book outline, this is a great time to share that with us as well. Finally, we give you instructions for sending us any audio files for review.

Your Feedback (Varies)

The amount of time you take to provide feedback on what we create for you is entirely up to you. Here's a quick breakdown as to when we'll ask you to provide feedback:

- When we send you a writing sample,
- When we send you the first full draft for review,
- When we send you your final proof.

Book Launch (Varies)

We celebrate your accomplishment, gain exposure, capitalize on media attention, and make sales!

Earning the Amazon best-seller badge in your subcategory helps you maximize your leverage. If positioned correctly, it snatches the attention of conferences, podcasts, and media outlets.

You can do several tasks that optimize your launch, including (but not limited to):

- Coordinating a live book-launch party
- Gathering a review team to read your book and leave their honest reviews
- Asking for endorsements
- Landing speaking engagements about your given topic

Meet Caleb Breakey

Traditional Publishing Broke His Heart, So He Set Out to Create a New Advantage for Authors.

Caleb Breakey and his wife began their married life by purchasing more than 50 books about writing. The newlyweds would often pen stories for hours at a time while serving as live-in night managers at a retirement facility.

Caleb spent the next decade breaking into the traditional publishing industry. He sold 20,000 books but found himself unsatisfied with the results. So, he took a four-year break to learn marketing secrets from a mentor who'd spent $1 billion in advertising. What good is a message, after all, if you can't get it out to the world? Now he's helped hundreds of aspiring authors write books, build platforms, and win book contracts.

The words Caleb longs to hear at the end of his life were penned many hundreds of years before his birth in Numbers 14:24 (NKJV): *"But My servant Caleb, because he has a different spirit in him and has followed Me fully, I will bring into the land."*

He lives in Washington State with his wife, Brittney, and enjoys visits from two mischievous mini huskies and a smiley Shiba Inu.

Caleb's Accolades Include

- Wrote, edited, and worked on dozens of best-selling books (including New York Times, Wall Street Journal, USA Today, and the #1 book on all of Amazon)

- Empowered hundreds of authors through his companies Speak It To Book and Sermon To Book

- Penned a non-fiction manuscript that was named a Christian Book Award finalist by the Evangelical Christian Publishers Association

- Won the American Christian Fiction Writers Genesis Award for fiction writing

- Graduated from the Christian Writers Guild's Craftsman Course

- Earned the prestigious 2 Comma Award via the marketing platform Click-Funnels.

- Featured in Better Business Bureau, Outreach Magazine, Conscious Millionaire, Pro Church Tools, Your First Thousand Clients, and Christianity Today

- Taught at writing conferences across the nation, including Mount Hermon, Blue Ridge, Realm Makers, and numerous others

What Others Are Saying About Caleb

Every now and then an author like Caleb comes along who makes me say, "Where have you been!"
—**James L. Rubart**, *5-time Christy Award Winner*

Caleb is quite a creative guy.
—**Jerry B. Jenkins**, *NYT best-selling author of the Left Behind series*

Caleb's passion for storytelling reminds me of a comet: rarely seen, white-hot, and a bit dangerous.
—**Kevin S. Kaiser**, *writer and former brand strategist for NYT best-selling author Ted Dekker*

Made in the USA
Middletown, DE
02 September 2021

46749741R00022